TRACKED VEHICLES

The Army Library

TRACKED VEHICLES

by John Nicholas

Rourke Enterprises, Inc.
Vero Beach, Florida 32964

Tracked vehicles are the only means by which military forces can move rapidly across rough ground, muddy fields, and sandy shores.

C3

Library of Congress Cataloging-in-Publication Data
Nicholas, John, 1944-
    Tracked vehicles/by John Nicholas.
    p. cm. — (The Army library)
    Includes index.
    Summary: Describes different kinds of tracked vehicles used by the United States Army at various times in history, including tanks, armored recovery vehicles, and earthmovers.
    ISBN 0-86592-422-8
    1. Vehicles, Military — United States — Juvenile literature. 2. Tracklaying vehicles — Juvenile literature. 3. United States.Army — Equipment — Juvenile literature. [1. Vehicles, Military. 2. Tracklaying vehicles. 3. United States. Army — Equipment.]
I. Title. II. Series: Nicholas, John , 1944- Army library.
UG618.N53   1989   623.74'7-dc19   88-13802
                                               CIP
                                               AC

CONTENTS

WHY TRACKS?

No one knows who invented the wheel. It has existed for a very long time, probably more than 6,000 years. When it was invented, however, the wheel revolutionized transportation and the movement of men and supplies. No longer was the load restricted to the amount a single animal could carry on its back. The horse could now be used to pull loads much heavier than it could carry. The wheel opened the way for the widespread movement of people and things on a large scale and helped expand civilization.

The wheel had only one drawback. It required a relatively level surface and solid ground to operate well. If rain or flood turned pathways into mud and sludge, the wheel was soon helpless and became stuck in the wet ground. This happened because all the weight was resting on the small area of wheel that actually touched the surface.

Tracks are used for almost every conceivable type of army vehicle, including light tanks and anti-aircraft guns.

Tracks allow this Marda mechanized infantry vehicle to move quickly across land and provide an escort for main battle tanks. Their job is to fight off anti-tank troops, leaving the big tanks free to attack heavily defended targets.

Tracks enable tanks to move quickly from place to place across difficult terrain and bring fire power to bear upon enemy forces. ▼

Imagine a 15-ton truck with four wheels. The total surface area of four tires resting on the ground can be as little as 150 square inches. That means that each square inch is supporting 200 pounds in weight! This will not be a problem if the ground is solid and able to support that amount of weight. One square inch is a very small area, and 200 pounds is more than the weight of a fully grown man. If the road surface turns to mud, the wheel starts to sink in and will soon get stuck.

For some time there seemed to be no solution to the problem. Then, nearly 4,500 years ago, the Egyptians needed to move giant stones weighing several tons to build the pyramids. There were no engines in those days, and everything that moved did so because of human or animal muscle. So to distribute the weight of those giant stones, the ancient Egyptians used rollers. These not only provided a surface on which to push the stones, but also spread the stones' weight, which prevented them from digging into soft ground.

What the Egyptians did in ancient times the modern army has modified to perfection. Soldiers know that battlefields are not paved with concrete and dry land. Wars are fought in fields and jungles as well as in towns and villages. The paved roads that connect cities are not necessarily the routes taken by invading armies. In World War One (1914-18), millions of men were confined to trenches and holes and never saw a paved road.

Because tanks can go where wheeled vehicles cannot, anti-tank missile systems carried on vehicles like this Jaguar also need tracks.

It was during World War One that the first military tracked vehicles were developed. Known as tanks, they began a completely new way of fighting and resulted in a new form of warfare, **blitzkrieg**. *Blitzkrieg* is a German word meaning "lightning war," and describes a war technique in which numerous tanks and vehicles move quickly through the countryside smashing everything that lies in their way. Supported by dive bombers, this was the method of warfare used by the German Nazi leader Adolf Hitler when he raced through Europe in 1939 and 1940.

The first commercial tracked vehicle was built in 1906 by the American Holt Manufacturing Company. They converted a steam-driven tractor to open up new territory for agriculture, away from prepared tracks. During World War One the British and the Germans used tanks to crush barbed wire and trample across trenches. The soldiers inside the tanks were protected from the bullets of enemy machine guns by armor plate.

By World War Two (1939-45), the old method of putting soldiers into trenches to hold certain positions had been transformed. Battles were fought on the move, with lots of vehicles involved to support the infantry. Even the big guns had become mobile, and tanks were built for speed, maneuverability, and the power of their guns. The development of the tank and the production of large tracked vehicles of this type led to a wide range of tracked vehicles to do many jobs on the battlefield.

The main battle tank is the most widely recognized tracked army vehicle and military forces throughout the world put great emphasis on its extraordinary capabilities.

The modern battle tank can move quickly over rough and muddy fields because its weight is distributed along the entire length of track in contact with the ground. For a tank like the M1 Abrams, each track is 2 feet wide and the length in contact with the ground is 15 feet. With two tracks, that totals 60 square feet, or 8,640 square inches. Because the tank weighs approximately 60 tons, each square inch of track carries less than 14 pounds weight to the ground. This gives the massive tank improved performance over poor ground conditions.

Tracks are really wheels that lay their own road as they go, spreading the weight of the vehicle over its full length on each ▶ side.

Tracked vehicles are also used to move infantry around; ◀ vehicles like this M113 can rapidly transport troops across the battlefield.

Tanks are mobile, fast, and can bring devastating fire power to other tanks and vehicles. ▼

RECOVERING THE WRECKS

Despite their heavy armor and robust design, tanks are vulnerable to attack from other tanks and anti-tank weapons. When they are hit by missiles or gunfire, they are not always destroyed, but sometimes just disabled. Their tracks may be broken, wheels may be blown off by shells, or some part of the engine or **transmission** might be hit. If recovered, the tanks can be repaired and returned to fight again.

Tank recovery and repair is an important task that keeps the army equipped in wartime. Most **armored recovery vehicles** are based on tank designs themselves. The standard medium recovery vehicle during the 1950s was the M74. It was based on the chassis of the old Sherman tank of World War Two. It was reliable but it did not have the ability to handle the heavier tanks that were then coming into service.

The M74 was based on old technology, because it used the chassis of an outdated tank hull. An attempt was made to turn it into a workable vehicle by replacing the gun turret with a fixed A-frame hoist attached to the front of the hull. A dozer blade at the front helped prevent the vehicle from tipping forward when the hoist was used. The vehicle had two winches in addition to numerous tools and spare parts in bins hung on the sides of the vehicle.

Tanks get a rough workout during training exercises and have a tough time in battle, where considerable damage can be inflicted by enemy guns, rockets, and missiles.

The M88 medium recovery vehicle was developed during the late 1950s; about a thousand vehicles of this type were built between 1961 and 1964.

The M74 was 26 feet long, 10 feet, 2 inches wide, and weighed 46 tons fully loaded. It was powered by a 450-horsepower engine which gave the M74 a speed of 21 MPH and a range of 100 miles. A single 7.62mm machine gun was carried for defense against aircraft or other light vehicles. The four-person crew was moderately protected from light gunfire, and the vehicle had unusually wide tracks to improve traction in poor ground conditions.

During 1954, work on a new medium recovery vehicle got under way and three prototypes, called the T88, were put together by Bowen-McLaughlin-York. After the company held several trials and put together some pre-production machines, they required a contract to build the M88, as it was then called. Between 1961 and 1964, about 1,000 vehicles of this type were built, and some were exported to foreign countries. The M88 is now the standard armored recovery vehicle for tanks like the M1 Abrams and the M60, for **armored personnel carriers**, and for heavy **self-propelled artillery**.

The M578 went into production in 1962 and presently serves with artillery battalions, armored cavalry regiments, and infantry units.

The M88's hull is made of cast armor, and the crew members are well protected from small arms and shell splinters. The four crew members ride in the front and include the commander, driver, co-driver, and a mechanic. At the front of the vehicle, a hydraulically operated dozer blade can push debris and other obstacles out of the way. It can also be pushed into the ground to help stabilize the vehicle when the crane, mounted at the rear, is being used to lift vehicles.

The crane is actually an A-shaped frame, pivoted at the front of the vehicle with two long arms that rest across the top of the M88. With the dozer blade in the lowered position, this frame crane can lift up to 25 tons. Two winches are fitted under the crew compartment. The main winch has 200 feet of 32mm cable and can haul weights of up to 45 tons. The second winch is used for hoisting and has 200 feet of 16mm cable. The M88 carries many different tools and has an **auxiliary fuel pump** for transferring fuel to another vehicle.

The M578 crane can lift over seven tons and has a winch with more than 220 feet of cable.

The lighter M578 was developed from a chassis designed for self-propelled howitzers and brought into service at about the same time as the M88. ▼

The latest version, the M88A1, has a Continental diesel engine developing 750 horsepower. With this the vehicle has a road speed of up to 26 MPH and a range of 280 miles. Tow speed with a load is about 18 MPH. Without dozer blade it is 27 feet long, 11 feet wide, and just over 10 feet high to the top of the 0.5-inch anti-aircraft machine gun. The M88 weighs about 55 tons. Still another improved version with a more powerful engine, winch power, and crew protection is being built for the U.S. Army. Called the M88A2, it will appear in service during the 1990s.

Developed and brought into production about the same time as the M88, the M578 is a light armored recovery vehicle built by the Pacific Car and Foundry Company of Renton, Washington. It began life as the chassis for three separate weapons: the 175mm M107 and 203mm M110 self-propelled **howitzers** and the T245, which was a 55mm howitzer that never got past the prototype stage. In 1957, designers decided to use the basic chassis from these two self-propelled guns to produce the M578 recovery vehicle, which entered production for the army in 1962.

The driving position in the M578 is in approximately the same location as the driver's compartment on a tank.

The M578 is used to recover disabled M107 and M110 howitzers and serves widely with artillery battalions, armored cavalry regiments, and mechanized infantry units. It is also used to deliver spare parts, including engines and tank barrels, to armored units on the battlefield and to provide a hoist for taking out the old unit and putting in the new one. To do this, the M578 has a crane mounted at the rear. The crane can lift up to 7.5 tons, and the main winch carries a reel of 25mm cable 229 feet in length.

A large spade mounted at the rear digs into the ground to give the vehicle stability when the hoist is operating. The vehicle can tow up to 30 tons, which is useful for disabled armored personnel carriers and light fighting vehicles but not big tanks. The M578 is 21 feet, 6 inches long, 10 feet wide, and 11 feet high to the single machine

Retrieving damaged vehicles from the battlefield, repairing them, and bringing them back into the fight is an important part of maintaining the appropriate quantity of military equipment in the field.

gun on top. The vehicle weighs 26 tons and is powered by a 425-horsepower General Motors diesel engine. This gives it a top speed of 34 MPH and a range of 450 miles.

▲
Recovery vehicles are moved around on other vehicles to quickly position them where they are needed; some even travel by hovercraft from supply ship to shoreline.

Without tracks, the difficult job of pulling disabled vehicles out of muddy and hilly terrain would be virtually impossible. ▼

ON THE BATTLEFIELD

Armored recovery vehicles play a vital role on and off the battlefield. They remove disabled tanks, guns, and personnel carriers, provide spare engines, gun barrels, and a host of minor systems that can fail or be put out of action by enemy gunfire. Certain other vehicles exist solely to direct support operations on the battlefield. One of these demolishes obstacles that prevent tanks, other vehicles, or infantry from moving forward. Other vehicles include earth movers, artillery support vehicles, mine layers, and robots.

Officially called a **combat engineer vehicle**, the M728 is similar to the medium armored recovery vehicle described in the previous section. Like the M74, it is a tank chassis that has been converted and modified to carry out

Troops like these depend on having well maintained tracked vehicles to support a forward thrust or to carry them to safety in the event of a surge attack by the enemy.

tough jobs in rough country. It is based on the M60A1 battle tank, of which the U.S. Army has about 7,300 in service. The hull is fitted with a hydraulically operated bulldozer blade, and an A-frame hoist is usually folded down around the sides of the turret.

A view of a fully tracked M728 combat engineer vehicle, equipped with bulldozer blade and a 165mm cannon.

Unlike the recovery vehicles, the M728 retains its gun turret, and the vehicle is armed with a 165mm low-speed **demolition gun**. Shells from this gun blow apart obstacles or buildings, and the dozer blade is used to clear a path. The hoist can lift a maximum load of 12 tons. The M728 is used for a wide variety of jobs, from blasting open roadways for light vehicles to hauling away the remains of destroyed enemy tanks and guns.

The M728 has a length of 25 feet, 10 inches and is 12 feet, 2 inches wide. It weighs 57 tons, carries a crew of four and is powered by a 750 horsepower Continental diesel engine. It has a top speed of 30 MPH and a range of 310 miles. Like the M60 from which it has been developed, the vehicle is made by the Chrysler Corporation in Detroit, Michigan.

A replacement for the M728 has beeen developed and will reach the army during the 1990s. Called a **counter-obstacle vehicle (COV)** its several roles and

responsibilities include all jobs the M728 can do plus mine clearing. The COV has been developed at the Belvoir Research, Development, and Engineering Center in Fort Belvoir, Virginia. It is powered by a 908-horsepower, twin turbo-charged diesel engine and is one of the most powerful vehicles operated by the army.

The COV is equipped with a dozer 15 feet wide capable of clearing earth and mines for a free vehicle pathway. It has two enormous telescopic arms, each extending to 32 feet with up to four different tools fitted to the end. With a bucket on each arm, the vehicle can move 160 cubic yards of earth per hour. Each bucket is 5 feet wide and digs out objects from the ground or clears debris and wreckage.

Other tools include a grapple, an impact hammer, and an auger. The impact hammer can pound the ground with a 600-pound blow. The auger is like a giant screw and can bore a hole quickly. The arms can be used to lift objects, each one having the capacity to raise 7.5 tons with the arm

A group of M88 heavy recovery vehicles awaits shipment to some foreign destination.

retracted, or about 4 tons with the arm extended. The dozer blade can be set to clear a specific depth of earth, thus moving aside mines that would destroy or damage light vehicles and personnel carriers.

Earth movers play an important part in clearing the ground. The latest in use with the army is the M9. This is fast enough to move with the tanks and tough enough to live and fight with the infantry. The M9 can work closer to the forward edge of the battle than previous earth movers, because it has adequate protection and armor to survive. Its job is to fill craters and ditches, help fighting vehicles, remove road blocks, trees, and rubble, prepare river crossings, and maintain combat routes for armor and supply vehicles.

The vehicle has an unusual type of suspension that allows the vehicle chassis to tip, tilt, raise, or lower the main body. This helps it adapt to the ground better and allows it to position the enormous dozer blade for the job. It can speed across country at up to 30 MPH and take on ballast to make it stable when moving earth. The M9 has a maximum weight of 27 tons and can be transported by air in C-130 Hercules or Lockheed C-141 Starlifter cargo planes.

Heavily armored for operating in the thick of battle, this M9 armored combat earth mover is designed to fill craters and ditches, smash road blocks, clear rubble, and keep a path open for fast-moving tracked wheeled combat vehicles.

Bulldozers are vital for clearing rubble from the scene of battle, keeping pathways and roads clear for heavy traffic.

Support vehicles with rollers and scrapers are vital for preparing operational bases and landing strips. ▼

Together, the COV and the M9 will put muscle on the battlefield for a host of rough, tough, and dirty jobs essential to keep the tanks rolling and the infantry moving. The artillery is served particularly by some very special vehicles that help coordinate land forces. One, called the fire support team vehicle, or FISTV, is based on the chassis of the M113A2 armored personnel carrier and is known in the army as the M981.

This vehicle directs artillery and mortar fire onto enemy targets, helping to improve the accuracy of guns and shells as they fire forward out of sight. The M981 carries observers on board who use special sensors to measure the accuracy of the artillerymen's fire. They report the results back to the field battery. A laser device pinpoints the target and sends accurate measurements to the guns to improve the aim.

The M981 consists of a standard M113 body with the special sensor pods on top. It weighs 13 tons and has a top speed of 19 MPH across rough country, with a range of 300 miles. A single 7.62mm machine gun protects the light vehicle and its four crew members against air attack, and sophisticated communications equipment allows the crew to keep in touch with artillery command posts and

On shore, dozers moving easily on tracks help maintain a constant flow of stores and ammunition on and off ships.

Not all army support vehicles operate on tracks; these are moved quickly from place to place by the army's heavy vehicle ▶ transporters.

firing units. The vehicle uses a **satellite navigation system** that tells it precisely where it is. This helps generate target-ranging information back to the guns.

Artillerymen on the battlefield have difficulty keeping supplies of ammunition on hand. As artillery has become more powerful, rates of fire have increased dramatically, which means that more ammunition is used up. The guns themselves have became much more mobile, adding the logistical problem of delivering ammunition supplies. In addition the **caliber**, or internal barrel diameter, of the guns is larger, and therefore the rounds of ammunition are larger and heavier. Fewer shells can be carried with the guns.

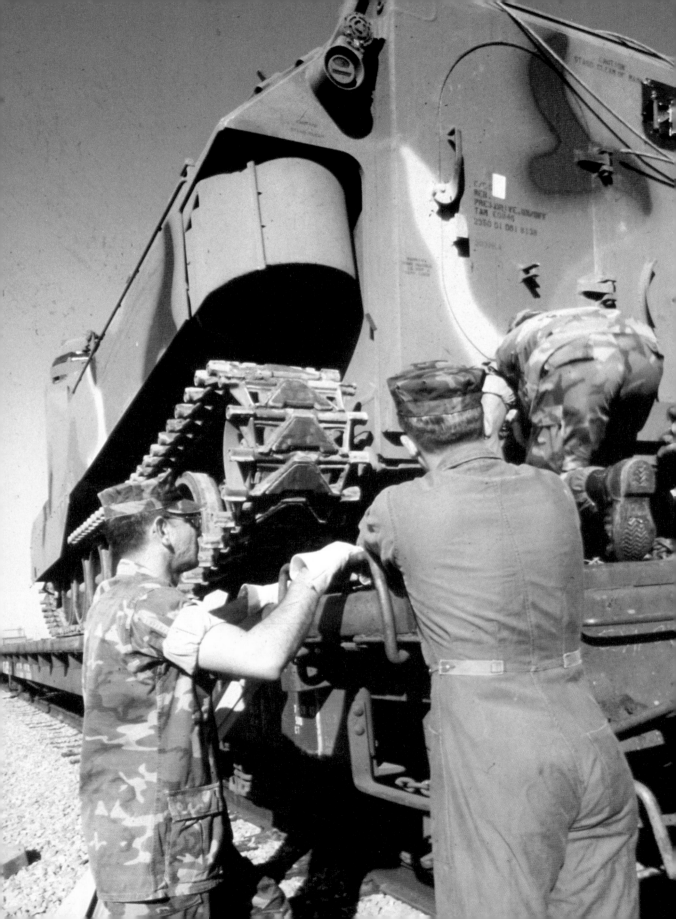

Roads and prepared pathways are usually left for infantry and wheeled vehicles, which cannot take the shorter routes across ▶ country.

Sometimes the recovery vehicles must rescue broken-down ◀ tracked vehicles, which are then quickly taken from the area of combat by road or rail.

An M1 Abrams main battle tank at speed during exercise Bright Star in 1987. ▼

Converted tanks are frequently used for mine clearing, road rolling, and for pushing aside obstacles in the path of following traffic.

Until the introduction of a special **ammunition support vehicle**, the guns were supplied by convoys of trucks such as the M548 cargo carrier and 5-ton vehicles with little or no protection for the crew. Unloading rounds of ammunition was a tiring job full of danger. To change this, the army has developed the M992 field artillery ammunition support vehicle. The M992 can keep the larger guns supplied on a regular basis.

The vehicle itself was developed from the basic design for the M109 self-propelled howitzer. It supports both this and the 203mm self-propelled howitzer. In place of the M109 turret with its 155mm gun, the supply vehicle has an armored housing capable of containing and transporting 48 203mm rounds or 93 155mm projectiles and the necessary fuses. Rounds are loaded aboard the vehicle at the ammunition dump using a special hoist with a 1,500-pound lifting capacity.

When the M992 arrives at the field battery it backs up to the howitzer and opens the rear door at the back of its armored housing. A special stacking device inside the supply vehicle lifts projectiles from their stowed positions, connects them to their charges and fuses, and feeds them to a special hydraulic conveyer. The conveyer automatically feeds the assembled rounds to the howitzer at a rate of 6 per minute. This is twice the firing capacity of the gun, so the supply vehicle does not restrict the use of the howitzer.

In all, the vehicle can carry 7.5 tons of cargo, about 6 tons of which is ammunition, and it can move at 35 MPH on paved roads. The M992 is 22 feet, 3 inches long and 10 feet, 10 inches wide. It is 10 feet, 8 inches high and weighs almost 29 tons fully loaded. Power is provided by a 405-horsepower turbo-charged diesel engine, and the vehicle has an unrefueled range of approximately 220 miles. It has sufficient armor to protect the crew from small arms and shell fragments, and it is equipped to operate in an environment where nuclear, biological, or chemical weapons are being used.

The U.S. Army wanted about 1,400 M992 support vehicles, and by the late 1980s about 520 had been delivered. More may be purchased in the 1990s to help improve the performance of the big howitzers. So far, all the vehicles built have been equipped to handle 155mm ammunition, but tests are being carried out on the version designed to carry and deliver 203mm rounds for the M110 self-propelled gun.

Light, wheeled recovery vehicles move quickly along prepared roads and help lift heavy supplies and ammunition crates.

One weapon that has always attracted those whose job is to devise ways of halting armored columns is the mine, a device concealed on the ground and designed to explode when a vehicle passes over it. In practice, however, the mine has never really achieved widespread use. This is probably because mines cannot be laid in peace time, and the time taken to deploy them takes people away from important duties close to the battle area.

Because the Soviets built large numbers of powerful tanks, the U.S. Army sought ways to stop them if they ever attacked European countries. The mine seemed to be an obvious answer. It was effective and relatively cheap to buy in the large numbers necessary to stop tank columns. To speed up the mine-laying process, the army developed its ground-emplaced mine-scattering system **(GEMSS)**. The GEMSS is a mine dispenser mounted on an M794 trailer towed by one of several tracked vehicles, including the M548 cargo carrier or the M113 armored personnel carrier.

Tracked dozers are useful for moving barrels of gasoline, water, or liquid explosive.

Because tracked vehicles easily tear up paved surfaces, wheeled vehicles are used for laying down new roads and airstrips where an even surface is essential.

This Soviet tracked vehicle is a trench-digging machine that can rapidly provide cover for infantry and support troops. ▶

The M128 mine dispenser holds up to 800 4-pound mines, which are deployed at intervals. Depending on the speed of the vehicle towing the trailer, the mines can be laid at intervals of anywhere from 96 feet to 192 feet. The M128 can carry various mines, including **magnetic influence mines** that are triggered by the presence of an armored vehicle. As long as friendly forces know where the minefield is, only enemy vehicles are blown up.

Another mine carried by the GEMSS is an anti-personnel fragmentation device designed to kill people rather than to destroy vehicles. Trip wires trigger it when a human foot or ankle disturbs the wire. Mines like these cannot easily be cleared from fields where they have been sown. They have anti-disturbance devices that trigger them if anyone tries to clear them up.

The army has just over 100 GEMSS vehicles that can be deployed with units as necessary, but it is also studying a mine-clearing device. Called **ROBAT**, for robotic obstacle-breaching assault tank, the vehicle is being developed at the Army Tank-Automotive Command's

Unimog, the ultimate wheeled trenching, dozing, lifting, and leveling machine.

Research and Development Center. The prototype, a converted M60A3 tank, is being used to develop and test equipment that will lead to a fully automated system for future applications.

The ROBAT vehicle would be driven by a crew of two, who would take it to the edge of the minefield and prepare it for remote-controlled operation. Pulling out the remote-control equipment, the crewmen would find a place to hide while overlooking the whole area. They would then command the tank through a small TV screen linked to a special receiver. A camera on the ROBAT sends pictures back to the operators who "drive" the vehicle through the minefield.

ROBAT destroys mines by launching rocket-propelled lines of explosives that trigger the mines and blow them up. The ROBAT would be amored underneath to withstand nearby explosions but the intention is to detonate the field of mines in one attempt. A clever device lays a trail of luminous candles, showing field troops where the ROBAT has been and where the safe areas are.

Tanks are best operated in squadrons where several are involved in a single action or in groups where support vehicles can readily service the needs of battle-damaged tanks.

BRIDGE LAYERS

Recovery vehicle support troops pause to assign their vehicles positions close to the battlefield.

The movement of troops and infantry divisions across broad areas of open country means that sooner or later they will come to a river. Small boats and inflatable dinghies are sufficient to move a few men over narrow strips of water, but wars today are fought primarily with many troops and much equipment. Tanks, guns, howitzers, and armored personnel carriers do not usually float.

The enormous increase in mechanized army units provides opportunities for advance and assault that soldiers could only dream of in World War Two. One result is that the modern army needs a steady stream of supplies — fuel, lubricants, oil, water, food, medical supplies, clothing, ammunition, and a wide range of small support items.

These supplies, or logistics, can only move when the means exists to transport them. The modern battlefield army units need the means to cross rivers with tanks, guns, and artillery as well as all the logistics supply and support vehicles. During World War Two the U.S. met this problem by using tank chassis, suitably modified, serving as bridge layers.

Bridges must be put down quickly and reliably. This usually falls to the army engineers. The enemy may have blown up existing bridges or, as is usually the case, existing bridges are nowhere near the place the army wants to cross.

The standard M60 battle tank has formed the base on which has been developed the M60 armored-vehicle-launched bridge (**AVLB**). It followed the M48 AVLB based on the medium tank developed in the early 1950s. The M60 AVLB is essentially the chassis and lower body of the original tank but with special bridge-laying devices on top and a bridge in folded sections to reduce its length when traveling.

The M60 armored-vehicle-launched bridge (AVLB) has been developed from the M60 battle tank; it uses powerful hydraulic jacks to raise the two sections of a hinged bridge.

Tracked bridge-laying vehicles are frequently the only means by which streams and rivers can be paved with a ready-made road essential for the fast flow of supplies. ▼

This vehicle uses bridges in two sizes. One weighs 16 tons and is made of aluminum, which combines lightness with strength. Unfolded, the bridge is 63 feet long and can span a river 60 feet across within three minutes. It takes up to one hour to pack up the bridge and reattach it to the M60. The second bridge weighs 9.5 tons and is also made of aluminum. It has an unfolded length of 92 feet, 10 inches and can span 88 feet, 7 inches. Both bridges are designated Type 60, which means they can each support 60-ton weights.

On the road, the M60 AVLB weighs 46 tons and is powered by a Continental diesel engine that delivers 750 horsepower. This gives it a top speed of 30 MPH and a range of 310 miles. The vehicle is 28 feet, 4 inches long and has a width of 12 feet with a total height of 10 feet, 4 inches. It has no armament, a crew of two, and a limited amount of armor protection.

The recent production of heavy tanks and more advanced fighting vehicles has made the M60 obsolete. It is being replaced with the Heavy Assault Bridge (**HAB**). HAB can lay a bridge 106 feet in length, 13.5 feet in width, with a clear roadway 13 feet across. Moreover, when packed for traveling, the bridge is 44 feet, 7 inches long, 13 feet, 6 inches wide, and 13 feet high. The maximum time to put down the bridge is five minutes, and the maximum time to recover is ten minutes.

HAB is based on the M1 Abrams main battle tank and weighs approximately 63 tons. A specially adapted system using hydraulics and jacks lays the bridge quickly and effectively. The bridge is a Type 70, which means it can support 70 tons weight, which will accommodate the heavier tanks. A special version of the HAB will be made for remaining M60 tanks in service. The first prototype M1 conversion was completed in May 1986, and tests have begun before production gets under way for the 1990s.

◄ *The bridge laid by the M60 AVLB has an unfolded length of almost 93 feet and can support 60 tons.*

Supply vehicles, infantry vehicles, and even tanks would be unable to cross many obstacles without special bridge-laying equipment. ▼

▲
M60 bridge-laying vehicles have an un-refueled range of more than 300 miles.

The M60 AVLB weighs 46 tons and is powered by a 750-horsepower diesel engine that gives it a top speed of 30 MPH. ▼

The army is now developing a larger bridge-layer based on the M1 Abrams main battle tank, which will enter service in the ▶ *1990s.*

GOING PLACES

Not every army vehicle needs brute force and sheer power. Sometimes, the fighting man must go where normal operating conditions are difficult and hazardous. Year-round operations in Arctic conditions, for instance, call for a very special type of vehicle. Such is the M973, a support vehicle on tracks. It is built to cross very rough country and operate on snow or ice in sub-zero temperatures. Moreover, it is capable of being flown in by air or lifted by helicopter.

The M973 is actually two vehicles: a forward, motorized driving tractor and a rear car for carrying supplies and small quantities of cargo. This cargo consists of subsistence equipment such as food, clothing, or small quantities of ammunition. The design of the vehicle allows it to operate in rocky or mountainous terrain as well as the wet and the cold. Not surprisingly, the M973 was designed and built in Sweden, where people are used to those sorts of conditions.

The forward tractor has a **curb weight** of 5,500 pounds, or about 2.75 tons. When packed with a maximum load of 1,300 pounds, its gross weight is 6,800 pounds. The vehicle can carry five passengers in addition

to the driver, and it has 88 cubic feet of cargo space. The rear car can carry 3,100 pounds of cargo on a curb weight of 3,700 pounds so the total weight is the same as the tractor's. It has 194 cubic feet of storage volume and can carry eleven people.

Connected together, the two sections of the vehicle are 22 feet, 6 inches in length, with a width of 6 feet and a height of 7 feet, 9 inches. It has a maximum speed of 31 MPH along paved roads or 2 MPH in water. The vehicle is designed to float, and the motion of the tracks keeps it moving forward. This little vehicle has been used by the armies of the U.S., Canada, West Germany, Italy, Great Britain, Norway, Finland, Spain, and Sweden.

Small vehicles like the M973 are a vital element among the large number of tracked vehicles operated by the U.S. Army. They provide support for winter activity and keep remote outposts supplied and stocked. The army has wide responsibilities in many far-off places, and vehicles like these help it reach even the loneliest outpost

◄ *Sometimes tracked vehicles are directly off-loaded from beach landing ships.*

Small vehicles designed to support artillery fire and air defense systems must also go where wheeled vehicles would have difficulty. ▼

▲
Beach landing craft with water-tight engine and suspension systems use tracks for easy access to beaches and marshy ground.

In cold climates with snow and ice the tracked vehicle is essential for moving quickly across roads and fields.

THE FUTURE

Increasingly, the army has come to rely on tracked vehicles for all forms of warfare. During the two world wars, the tank was developed into a mature fighting vehicle. It was able to move where no wheeled vehicle had previously been able to go and at a speed which was unimaginable without powerful engines to drive them. As time went on, the concept of a mobile battlefield grew, until almost every type of weapon was put on tracks. Even the big guns of the army, the giant howitzers, were given mobility with large tracked bodies.

Now, to support those fighting vehicles, support and logistics vehicles have come to dominate supply and servicing. Everything that moves on the battlefields now runs on tracks, including small groups of infantrymen in armored fighting vehicles. In the future, increasing automation will add a new dimension to mobile warfare — robots.

Whatever developments lie ahead in modern battlefield technology, the tracked vehicle is here to stay for a very long time.

We have seen a beginning with the ROBAT mine-clearing vehicle used to fire strings of explosive charges. Engineers and designers are working on a range of remotely controlled tanks that can be operated by a "driver" sitting in protected cover several miles away. With television eyes and an electronic brain, the tank will go into the thickest part of the battle without fear. There is no living driver inside.

The use of robot tanks is only one way in which the modern battlefield will change. Artillery troops will need more and more ammunition, and support vehicles like the M992, which delivers rounds to the big howitzers, will be an essential part of rapid-fire barrages to hit enemy positions several miles away. Artillery fire is still one of the most important aspects of both attack and defense and is a fundamental activity of modern warfare.

The development of powerful engines and sophisticated electronics have improved the army's fighting vehicles. Still, military vehicles are continually looking for more efficient ways to support army operations. The existing fleet of support vehicles shows the wide range of applications the basic tracked vehicle has been called upon to perform. There is no sign that this role will diminish, and even more exotic designs are just around the corner.

There are always some places where neither tracked nor wheeled vehicles are able to go and, when troops move in those places, muscle power is often the only way to move small quantities of supplies and equipment. ▶

With their special rubber wheels, M759 cargo carriers travel easily across marshy land that even the lightest tracked recovery vehicles would find impossible. ▼

ABBREVIATIONS

AVLB   Armored-Vehicle-Launched Bridge

GEMSS   Ground-Emplaced Mine-Scattering System

HAB   Heavy Assault Bridge

ROBAT   Robotic Obstacle-Breaching Assault Tank

GLOSSARY

Ammunition support vehicle	A vehicle designed to carry shells to guns, cannon, or howitzers on the battlefield.
Armored personnel carriers	Tracked or wheeled vehicles protected with armor plate and used to carry soldiers or infantry men.
Armored recovery vehicles	Vehicles designed to recover damaged tanks and armored personnel carriers.
Auxiliary fuel pump	A fuel pump that transfers fuel from the tanks of one vehicle to the tanks of another vehicle via pipes or leads attached between the two.
Blitzkrieg	The German word for lightning war, the name given to surprise attack involving ground attack planes and tanks.
Caliber	The diameter of the inside of the barrel of a gun indicating the power of the artillery piece.
Combat engineer vehicle	A multi-purpose vehicle fitted with bulldozer blades, hoists, and other equipment for clearing debris from the battlefield.
Counter-Obstacle Vehicle (COV)	A multi-purpose vehicle designed to clear mines, detonate booby traps, and remove obstacles of all kinds.
Curb weight	The unloaded weight of a tank or tracked vehicle.
Demolition gun	A gun carried by an army vehicle to blast physical obstructions and clear a path for advancing vehicles.
Howitzer	A large gun or cannon that has short barrels for firing low-speed charges.
Magnetic influence mines	Mines that are triggered by the presence of an armored vehicle in the vicinity.
Satellite navigation system	A vehicle equipped with instruments to pick up signals from navigation satellites and obtain an indication of position.
Self-propelled artillery	Guns, cannons or howitzers that carry their own mode of propulsion and therefore do not have to be towed.
Transmission	The linkages, usually through a gearbox, connecting the engine with the drive shaft.

INDEX

Page references in *italics* indicate photographs or illustrations.